T HE GREAT RECESSION has exposed to public scrutiny the generous pay and benefits that many government employees receive. At a time when many states (to say nothing of that superstate, the federal government) are staggering under unprecedented debt, the Shangri-la of public-sector, government unions has aroused widespread criticism as well as the envy of average workers in the private sector. In February 2011, the newly elected Republican governor of Wisconsin, Scott Walker, gave voice to those resentments, saying, "We can no longer live in a society where the public employees are the haves and the taxpayers who foot the bill are the have-nots." Addressing the issue of fiscal continence as well as the issue of fairness, Walker sparked a national debate over the legitimacy and desirability of a unionized government workforce. His proposal called for the state's public employees to pay a bit more of their pension and health care costs (still less than the national average for government workers and far less than the private-sector average);

it rolled back collective-bargaining rights for most government workers; and it took the state out of the business of collecting union dues. Walker's proposals elicited a heated response from public employees and their Democratic allies. Some 60,000 protesters descended on the state Capitol in Madison, and teachers effectively went on strike for a couple days by calling in sick in large numbers. Democratic state senators fled to Illinois to prevent a vote on the measure. Even President Obama accused Walker of launching an "assault on unions." Nevertheless, after three weeks of fruitless negotiations with absentee Democrats, Walker and his Republican colleagues in the Legislature forged ahead and enacted significant changes to Wisconsin's public labor laws.

The steps taken by Wisconsin's Republican leaders have quickly been seconded in Ohio, where the state's governor, John Kasich, and the state Legislature are, as of this writing, close to passing similar measures. The legislative battles playing out in the Midwest follow on the heels of actions taken by New Jersey's hard-charging governor, Chris Christie, who improbably became a national celebrity through his battles with his state's public-employee unions. Christie targeted for reform the burdens that public workers' health and pension benefits place on the Garden State's long-term finances. He dared to propose measures that just yesterday were considered "impossible" or "political suicide." The teachers unions reacted with fury, spending millions on attack ads in 2010 to block Christie's proposals. Yet in cooperation with a state Legislature controlled by Democrats, Christie has changed pension rules, instituted a 2 percent property-tax cap, and required teachers to make small contributions to their health-insurance plans. He is now seeking to reform the teacher tenure system.

Other states – such as Nevada, Michigan, New York, California, and Pennsylvania – are also revisiting the status and role of unionized government workers in their politics. The reason for this wave of concern is that in the

In the past half-century, unions representing public servants have become political powerhouses.

---

past half-century, unions representing public servants have become political powerhouses. In recent campaigns and elections, they have provided large sums of money to candidates, almost all of it to Democrats, at all levels of government. They make huge independent expenditures on campaign ads, again almost always for Democratic candidates. In addition, they provide the foot soldiers for voter registration and get-out-the-vote drives. "We're the big dog," says Larry Scanlon, the political director of the American Federation of State, County, and Municipal Employees (AFSCME), the largest union of government workers in the country. AFSCME's website brags that candidates "all across the country, at every level of government" have learned to "pay attention to AFSCME's political muscle." And the union has used that formidable muscle to elect allies and secure generous pay and substantial benefits for their members at significant cost to taxpayers.

The main reason for the unions' success is that the political process affords public-sector unions much more influence over their members' employers – that is, the government – than private-sector unions could ever dream of. Government unions help elect politicians who then act as "management" in negotiations over pay, benefits, and work rules. "We elect our bosses, so we've got to elect politicians who support us," AFSCME's website flatly states. The result is a cycle that is hard to break. Unions extract dues from their members and funnel them into politicians' campaign war chests, then those same politicians agree to generous contracts for public workers – which in turn leads to more union dues, more campaign spending, and so on. It is a cycle that has dominated the politics of some of America's states with dire consequences.

The principal function of unions is to represent their members' interests. Therefore, those in the public sector have interpreted the reform proposals of Christie, Walker, and Kasich as a serious threat. Defenders of public-employee unions, like former Secretary of Labor Robert Reich, have charged that humble public workers are being targeted as "scapegoats" for the Great Recession. They argue that most government employees live modest lives and aren't paid better than workers in the private sector. Criticizing public servants, they say, only serves to divert attention from the corporate executives who perpetrated today's economic crisis. The unions help sustain a professional public service and preserve a segment of the hard-pressed middle class that would otherwise be thrust into a cruel race to the bottom. The arguments of the unions and their defenders have some merit. But ultimately, they are unpersuasive.

Attention to government unions has revealed two pressing problems: First, the unions exercise considerable political clout in a partially acknowledged symbiosis with the Democratic Party, and second, the economic consequences of that alliance are fiscally un - sustainable promises and inflexible government. These two interrelated problems were present before the financial crisis, but when it took the economic tide out, the strain on government finances and taxpayer wallets was readily apparent. In the wake of the Great Recession, it has become clear across the country that the road to genuine reform runs straight through these unions. How to deal with them and their Democratic allies presents state and local officials with a huge challenge that is likely to occupy them for years. But deal with them they must: Business as usual with public-sector unions has produced staggering government obligations. The stakes in these battles are high. They involve the long-term fiscal health of the nation, the balance of power between the nation's two political parties, and the government's efficiency and effectiveness. Ultimately, insofar as the fiscal health of the country is at stake, we are confronted with a threat to the power and prestige of the United States on the world stage.

THE TAKEOFF

The story of the American labor movement is a tale rich with the organizing struggles of miners, ladies' garment workers, and autoworkers. Today, however, the conventional wisdom is that organized labor in America has been enfeebled. The inability of President Barack Obama and large Democratic majorities in the 111th Congress to pass labor's highest legislative priority, the Employee Free Choice Act (often called "check card"), is supposedly indicative of unions' political impotence. In 1955, organized labor represented one-third of the nonagricultural workforce. Today, it represents only 12.3 percent – and only 6.9 percent of private-sector workers. While there is much to be said for the "union decline" thesis, most observers have greatly underestimated labor's political power because they have overlooked public-employee unions. In spite of declining private-sector union membership, the unique attributes of government unions have helped maintain labor's power in American politics. In 2009, a major barrier was breached. For the first time, more government employees (7.6 million) than private-sector employees (7.1 million) belonged to unions. And this was despite the fact that 83 percent of workers labor in the private economy, while 17 percent are in the public sector.

The stakes in these battles are high. They involve the long-term fiscal health of the nation, the balance of power between the nation's two political parties, and the government's efficiency and effectiveness.

Before 1960, few government workers were union members. Party machines or civil-service rules determined who worked for the government and what they did. Many states even had laws on the books that forbade government workers from joining unions. Even in places where joining a union was legal, union rights were highly restricted. Over the course of the 1960s and early 1970s, however, there was a largely unnoticed "rights revolution." Public-employee unions won the right to organize and bargain collectively – a legally enforced process that determines binding contractual agreements for the terms and conditions of employment – with various units of government. Today, all but 12 states have collective bargaining for at least some public servants (usually those in the protective services, such as police and firefighters), and in only five states is public-sector collective bargaining completely proscribed. The growth of public-employee unions surged. By 1980, 36 percent of public employees belonged to unions – a figure that has remained roughly stable ever since. Yet disparities in state and local laws mean that the percentage varies widely from state to state. New York is at the top of the heap with 69 percent of its state employees in unions, while many Southern states have membership rates below 10 percent.

That powerful government unions exist at all is a striking political development. The prevailing attitude among policymakers across the political spectrum was downright hostile well into the 1950s. President Franklin D. Roosevelt, one of labor's best friends, wrote in 1937 that "meticulous attention should be paid to the special relations and obligations of public servants to the public itself and to the Government.... The process of collective bargaining, as usually understood, cannot be transplanted into the public service." Other champions of organized labor thought the same way. The first president of the AFL-CIO, George Meany, believed it was "impossible to bargain collectively with the government." Meany and Roosevelt's reasoning was that the elected representatives of the people would be forced to share their governing authority with unelected union officials whom voters could not hold accountable. The integrity of democratic self-government would thus be compromised.

For government unions to emerge, two things had to happen. The first was the destruction of the party machines at the state and local levels. Machine control of government work increased turnover in public employment by hitching it to election results. Patronage appointees rarely developed a culture of professionalism. Reformers sought to take patronage away from party bosses and ward healers and reduce the politicization of government work by enacting civil-service laws. By the end of the 1950s, reformers had largely succeeded. The most important consequence of civil-service reform was that public employees gained nearly lifetime job security, which enhanced their collective-action incentives. These laws also lifted the floor of worker protections on which union-negotiated contracts built.

The second precondition was the solidification of the alliance between the Democratic Party and organized labor. Roosevelt's signing of the Wagner Act in 1935 married labor to the Democrats. Private-sector union membership surged. By midcentury, Democrats began to rely heavily on labor unions for both campaign financing and grassroots organizing. Therefore, both Democrats and labor had a strong incentive to increase the size of the labor movement. Government workers were the new recruits, especially as private-sector union membership declined.

To give government workers the incentive to join unions, a series of measures granting them collective-bargaining rights were passed. In 1958, New York City Mayor Robert Wagner Jr. issued Executive Order 49, known as "the little Wagner Act." In 1959, Wisconsin passed the first statewide collective-bargaining law for public employees. And in 1962, President John F. Kennedy issued Executive Order 10988, which reaffirmed the right of federal workers to organize and codified some workers' rights to bargain collectively. Over the next decade, other states and cities passed a host of laws providing public-employee unions with collective-bargaining rights. Consequently, as private-sector unions withered in the 1970s, government-union membership took off.

The growth of government workers inside

In spite of declining private-sector union membership, the unique attributes of government unions have helped maintain labor's power in American politics.

---

the labor movement's ranks produced a noticeable change in the demographic profile of union members. In the 1950s, the typical union member was a high school-educated white male who lived in a major city. Today, white-collar workers are a majority of union members, and gender parity has almost been achieved. A quarter of union members have college degrees, most live in the suburbs, and unions have become multiracial. The sort of jobs union members do has also drastically changed. Union members today are more likely to be teachers, police officers, or firefighters than they are to be electricians, iron workers, or coal miners. In sum, unions today represent a very different segment of the workforce than they did when America was the world's leading manufacturer.

The shift in the makeup of the labor movement has had an impact on public perceptions of it. In the 1950s, many families had at least one member who was in a union. Today, few Americans know anyone who belongs to a private-sector union. In 2009, just 48 percent of Americans approved of labor unions – the lowest percentage Gallup has recorded since

1937. Gallup reported that while two-thirds of the public believed unions were good for their members, 51 percent believed they were bad for the economy in general. And 62 percent said they felt that unions "mostly hurt" workers who were not members. These perceptions pose significant problems for the Democratic Party, which for much of the 20th century was the home of working-class voters and which today is deeply dependent on union campaign support. Consequently, while it is clearly not in the short-term interests of many Democratic incumbents, it might actually be in the party's long-term interests to distance itself from the public unions. They could then more easily claim to represent the interests of most workers, not just government ones.

THE GOVERNMENT–UNION ADVANTAGE

Once up and running, government unions became some of the most powerful interest

powerful influence on election outcomes. The hold the unions exerted on former New Jersey Governor Jon Corzine was suddenly dramatized when he addressed a Trenton rally of roughly 10,000 public workers in 2006 and blurted out, "We will fight for a fair contract!" Why was a multimillionaire self-financing candidate kowtowing to the unions? Because he was locked in a tight contest with insurgent Republican Chris Christie and needed their get-out-the-vote operation. Corzine knew that every vote would count. If the unions sat on their hands, he was done for. The point is that the political influence of the unions is compounded by their ability to mobilize voters for a specific candidate.

Government unions exercise their greatest influence, however, in low-turnout elections with limited media scrutiny – elections for school boards, for instance, and many elections for state and local offices. In addition, the millions spent by public-employee unions on ballot initiatives and referenda almost always support policy changes leading to higher taxes and bigger government. The California Teachers Association, for example, spent $57 million in 2005 to defeat referenda that would have reduced union power and limited government growth. In 2010, the Oregon Education Association and the SEIU contributed nearly three-quarters of the funds to the campaign in favor of ballot measures that raised taxes on businesses and individuals in Oregon. In San Francisco in fall 2010, there was also a ballot measure that, had it passed, would have required city workers to increase their contributions to their pension and health care plans. City-workers unions spent a million dollars in opposition, the Democratic County Central Committee told voters to not to support it, and Mayor Gavin Newsom said publicly that if it passed, he wouldn't implement it. The measure was defeated. (San Francisco currently spends more on pensions than on parks or its fire department.)

The power of government unions to decide election outcomes is magnified by the fact that in many jurisdictions, their members constitute a disproportionate slice of the electorate. Stanford University political scientist Terry Moe has documented this phenomenon in school-board elections across the country. School boards often form autonomous government units, and elections to them tend to be low profile. Average voters — especially those who are not parents with school-age children — are often poorly informed about the candidates and the issues in these races. Teachers unions, on the other hand, have a powerful interest in who wins these races. And since teachers themselves often make up a large share of the electorate, they are able to elect members of the school board who are be - holden to them.

In between elections, government unions have significant advantages over private-sector unions and other interest groups in lobbying for their interests. A profound difference between public- and private-sector collective bargaining is that private-sector unions have a natural adversary in the owners of the companies with whom they negotiate. When private-sector unions negotiate with owners, the owners always have the enticement of keeping profits for themselves. But government unions face no such opposition. In the public sector, there are no profits for managers to keep. There are only the deep pockets that belong to someone else: the taxpayers.

Market forces also provide a powerful check on unions in the private sector. If private-sector unions demand too much compensation, they risk making their employer uncompetitive vis-à-vis its rivals. Union members' jobs are thus on the line if the company loses market share. On the other hand, because the government is the monopoly provider of many services, the pressure to be efficient is greatly relaxed. Finally, amid the "creative destruction" of the market, companies regularly go out of business, which means that private-sector unions must constantly redouble their organizing efforts. The government, on the other hand, never goes out of business. Therefore, once a group of public employees has formed a union, the union persists. Not

> *A profound difference between public- and private-sector collective bargaining is that private-sector unions have a natural adversary in the owners of the companies with whom they negotiate.*

having to spend more on organizing frees up more scarce resources for political activity.

Government unions also have a number of advantages over regular interest groups. First, they have access to politicians through the collective-bargaining process. Other interest groups must fight for such access. Second, government unions have a constituent base that can easily be mobilized for electoral participation, while most other interest groups do not. Third, most interest groups dedicate a major portion of their administrative overhead to fundraising. Government unions, by contrast, enjoy a steady revenue stream from union dues. In fact, the government often collects the dues, which drastically reduces the unions' administrative costs. And such savings on overhead can be redirected into electioneering and lobbying.

In American government, political power is often obscurely apportioned. Therefore, beyond direct lobbying of elected officials, government unions have sought to form alliances with actuaries, pension-fund board members, and other little-known officials with power over issues of concern to them. It is through such channels that seemingly small changes in the fine print of pension and health care plans can end up having big consequences.

And if working quietly behind the scenes doesn't cut it, unions often go public to pressure legislators. The tactics include rallies at the state Capitol along with ads on television, radio, and the Internet. The governor of New York, Andrew Cuomo, described how government unions operated in the Empire State: "We've seen the same play run for 10 years. The governor announces the budget, unions come together, put $10 million in a bank account, run television ads against the governor. The governor's popularity drops; the governor's knees weaken; the governor falls to one knee, collapses, makes a deal."

Defenders of government-workers unions often point out that their political power is limited because strikes are illegal in all but two states. (Of course, that doesn't mean strikes haven't been called.) Yet despite being a potent weapon in industrial labor relations, the strike is not a weapon government unions need to exercise influence. This is because government unions replaced the strike with a process called binding arbitration. When the government and its unionized workers cannot come to an agreement, many states and cities require the dispute to be settled by a third party. The structure of the situation privileges the unions' position by giving the unions the incentive to keep their final offer high enough to ensure stalemate, with the understanding that an arbitrator will split the difference be - tween the two sides and thus award the union more than the government's last bid. In 1981, Coleman Young, then mayor of Detroit, re- marked, "We know that compulsory arbitra- tion destroys sensible fiscal management ... [and has] caused more damage to the public service in Detroit than the strikes [it was] designed to prevent."

All of these advantages make government unions a threat to the Madisonian system in which the clash of competing private interests normally conduces to the public interest. When one group has so many advantages over the others and is deeply embedded in one of the two major political parties, it threatens to overwhelm the public interest.

THE TAXPAYER'S BURDEN

Government unions' political power increases the cost of government – most obviously in the form of greater compensation for government workers. Scholars disagree about how best to measure the differences in compensation between public- and private-sector workers. Depending largely on actuarial assumptions related to the price of future benefits, some find government workers make more in total compensation; others find they make slightly less than private-sector employees. But there are a few points that elicit broad agreement. Generally speaking, the public sector provides a pay premium for jobs at the low end of the labor market, while the private sector pays more, sometimes fantastically so, at the high end. In addition, government workers tend to work fewer hours and have more vacation days per year. The private sector usually requires workers to be much more flexible and to work longer hours. Considering all jobs, government workers today earn more per hour, on average, in total compensation (wages and benefits) than workers in the private sector. It is not worth emphasizing the aggregate pay differential, however, since much of it is easily explained by demographic differences. There are more white-collar jobs in government, which means that public employees tend to be better educated. In addition, most public employees live in urban areas where the cost-of-living and salary scales are higher.

Not as easily captured in many comparable-worth studies are those government workers who lack counterparts in the private sector, such as policemen, firefighters, and corrections officers. And these are the workers who have used their unique status to leverage some of the best compensation packages. In Massachusetts, for instance, a number of state troopers make more in salary than the governor. And a few corrections officers in California can make more than $300,000 a year with overtime. While jobs that require the risk of life and limb merit greater compensation, collective-bargaining contracts have provided a sizeable bonus.

Another factor that drives up public-sector pay is the long tenure of many government workers. Staying in a job and accepting incremental raises drives the pay scale up. Turnover in the public workforce is very small compared with the private sector, which indicates that people feel comfortable in their jobs. This is measured by what economists call the "quit rate," which is when workers voluntarily leave their jobs. In 2009, the quit rate in the public sector was one-third that of the private sector. Put differently, many more people quit in the private sector than in the public sector. If public employment has such a good retention rate, it hardly seems that such workers are being exploited.

Ultimately, union wages and salaries are not out of line with pay in the private sector. That is partly because pay increases must be factored into the government's budgets each fiscal year. Therefore, when the road to bigger paychecks has been blocked, the unions have turned their attention to benefits. Because benefits are future compensation, they don't pose the same political costs for lawmakers. Indeed, a great deal of compensation for work in the public sector occurs after an employee

> *If public employment has such a good retention rate, it hardly seems that such workers are being exploited.*

has stopped working. The unions' most cherished benefit is the pension. In California, for example, state workers often retire at 55 with lifetime pensions that equal or exceed what they made on the job. This year, the Golden State is confronted with a $25.4 billion budget gap but will pay pensions of $100,000 or more annually to some 12,000 retirees.

Part of the explanation for the "pension tsunami" is that about 80 percent of public workers have "defined benefit" retirement plans. Under these plans, when an employee retires, he or she receives a pension on the basis of a formula. In many states and localities, that formula is 2.5 to 3 percent of a worker's average salary during their three highest-earning years, times the number of years worked. For example, in New York State, if a state worker whose top salary was $80,000 wanted to retire at 55 after working for 30 years, his pension benefit would be $4,000 a month, or $48,000 annually. If the worker was not a government employee, he or she would need nearly $1 million in savings to have the same monthly retirement income. Such defined benefit plans are now rare in the private sector (only 18 percent of workers have them). Most workers in the private sector instead rely on "defined contribution" plans, which are similar to a 401(k).

How, a reasonable citizen might ask, were lawmakers ever induced to make such promises? Easy. Lawmakers discovered that pension "sweeteners" could be very good politics – that is, "good" for their re-election. Unable to raise pay any higher, calculating politicians placated the unions with future pension commitments. The money is then allocated, but it doesn't have to be paid immediately. The bill comes due when they are long out of office. Politicians could also appear generous by providing public services to citizens without raising taxes to pay for them. And sleight-of-hand budgeting and rosy actuarial assumptions obscured the truth about the fiscal health of state pension funds. Consequently, legislators who got into bed with the unions also deserve a great deal of the blame for governments' fiscal straits.

The long-term problem is that government has become too big, too cumbersome, and too expensive. Northwestern University economist Joshua Rauh estimates the states' current pension liabilities at $3 *trillion*. Some states are worse off than others. Those with strong government-workers unions tend to have greater unfunded liabilities. The Pew Research Center offers a less drastic but still worrisome calculation (made before the recession) that the states are on the hook for $1 trillion in retiree pension and health care costs. However liabilities are calculated, many states cannot renege on many of the promises they've made, because pensions are guaranteed by their constitutions.

Unions and their supporters respond to such arguments by waving them away. They point out that pension payments only account for about 4 percent of the states' average spending. What's a measly 4 percent? But this figure by itself is misleading. Some states spend as much as 10 percent of their annual budgets on pensions. And because even that figure might seem low, it must be put in context. Major portions of the states' budgets are fixed by federal mandates and bond payments. The percentage of the budget in which lawmakers can actually exercise discretion is much smaller than it first appears. This makes that small percentage devoted to pensions loom much larger, especially when it is in - creasing. Combine that with health care commitments to retirees, and the percentage of revenue goes up even further.

For all the talk about how public employees' pension costs can "crowd out" other government priorities, it should not be forgotten that retiree health care costs do the same thing. The Pew Center on the States estimates that the states currently have a $550 billion unfunded liability for promised retired-employee health coverage besides Medicare. Consequently, in Massachusetts, hundreds of millions of dollars in school funding never reached a classroom because they have been used to pay for the health care of education workers. This sort of outcome helps explain why the major increases in spending on education in the past 30 years have had so little effect on student performance.

The result is that taxpayers don't receive more government services for the greater costs they are paying. One group of economists reports that "since 1950, state and local spending has grown ... fast enough to double the size of state and local government every 8 or 9 years." Such growth would be logical if it were improving infrastructure, because better roads, bridges, and mass-transit systems increase economic efficiency. But that hasn't happened. Spending on infrastructure has been flat as a percentage of GDP since 1950. The implication is that employee compensation has gobbled up most of the growth in state and local spending.

While the economic downturn of 2008–2011 has caused a fiscal calamity for states and cities, their budgets were fraught with problems long before the recession hit. As John Hood has pointed out in *National Affairs*, these were due to unsustainable public-employee pension obligations, excessive borrowing, and

---

Lawmakers discovered that pension "sweeteners" could be very good politics – that is, "good" for their re-election.

---

overly optimistic budgeting in years of relative prosperity. The basic consequence is that taxpayers are now stuck spending more – a lot more – for less. If a government must spend more on pensions and health care for its workers, it cannot spend more on schools, roads, and poor relief. As former California Governor Arnold Schwarzenegger's economic adviser David Crane has pointed out, pension and health care obligations to his state's employees threaten to "crowd out funding for many programs vital to the overwhelming majority of Californians," including "higher education, transit, and parks." In other words, the core functions people expect their governments to perform get short-changed. State and local governments are now confronted with the difficult choice of either raising taxes or making deep cuts to critical programs.

Reducing Government Performance

The rise of government unionism helps explain the distinct private and public "worlds of work," as Harvard policy scholar John

Donahue has put it. The former is ultracompetitive and the rewards highly unequal, while the latter still provides multiple protections and greater equality in the pay scale. Government unions have shaped the conditions of their members' employment in ways that shield them from the fierce struggle that rages in the private sector. In the private sector, intense competition, constant evaluation, long hours, and pay-for-performance standards are the norm. Comparatively speaking, the public sector is an oasis of stability.

The differences between public- and private-sector work stem in part from allowing public-employee unions to have a large say in setting the conditions under which they work. Negotiating work rules means that they have the power to shape the daily routines of public servants. Because government workers are, in effect, the face of government that most people see, what they do shapes how well the government performs. Unfortunately, they tend to make government less effective and more expensive. American government does not, therefore, spend taxpayers' dollars very efficiently. The World Economic Forum ranks America 68th in the world on this score.

Unions also negotiate salary scales, promotion schedules, and other aspects of the workplace. This makes government work more attractive for some people than for others. Given the pay premium at the low end of the labor market for government work, those with limited skills increasingly seek it out. At the high end of the labor market, which requires much schooling and long years of experience, the fact that government work is less well compensated than the private sector can make it less appealing. Some scholars argue that a "brain drain" occurs when talented people leave government work for the handsome salaries and plush offices they can secure in the private market. Some workers may also opt out of government work to avoid the slow promotion process that prevails in the public sector. And highly educated employees who decide to stay in government work can sometimes be less innovative and less willing to experiment than their private-sector brethren.

Because the task of unions is to represent all their members as equally as possible, negotiated work rules protect high-performing and underperforming workers alike. The problematic result is that it is difficult for agency managers to reassign workers and nearly impossible to fire bad public employees. The termination process is so drawn out and costly that many managers often forgo it. Speaking of his state's teacher-tenure provisions, Nevada Governor Brian Sandoval remarked, "It's practically impossible to remove an underperforming teacher under the system we have now." In the first decade of the 21st century, the Los Angeles school district spent $3.5 million to sack seven teachers (out of 33,000).

While many factors contribute to the performance of state and local government, government unions tend to reduce efficiency and introduce greater rigidity. The Pew Center on the States grades state government performance, and those that came out on top, such as

Virginia and Texas, prohibit collective bargaining in the public sector. States with powerful government unions, such as California, New Jersey, and Rhode Island, received some of the worst grades. The implication is that offering the leaders of public bureaucracies greater flexibility can produce positive results.

The Way Out

The struggles of the 1960s invigorated government unionism; the Great Recession may end up gutting it. Indeed, the next year is going to be an especially challenging one for state and local lawmakers throughout the country. Many are confronted with painful choices in order to close yawning budget gaps. There are two basic alternatives (which can be combined). One is to try to diminish government-union power through structural reforms – such as limiting or ending collective bargaining and stopping governments from collecting union dues – that would sever the problematic links between unions and elected officials. The other is to work within existing arrangements and seek concessions from the unions on pay, pensions, health care, and work rules.

In light of the threat posed by government unions to fiscal sanity and democratic self-government, some governors, notably in Wisconsin and Ohio, have adopted the first approach. They are rolling back the 1960s collective-bargaining-rights revolution by narrowing the subject of collective bargaining to wages only for most workers. Pension and health benefits will no longer be legally mandatory subjects of negotiation.

The hope is that this will give agency managers greater flexibility in determining benefits and how public servants do their jobs. The principal effect of these changes in collective-bargaining rights is likely to be lower pension and health care benefits for new employees, which can reduce long-term spending. And it will make it more difficult for unions to win back concessions made in hard economic times when growth returns.

Critics of Walker and Kasich argue that "basic democratic rights" are being taken away. If they were so fundamental, however, all government workers would have them. But many don't. Texas, Virginia, North Carolina, South Carolina, and Georgia prohibit all collective bargaining with government-workers unions. Twelve other states only grant certain

The struggles of the 1960s invigorated government unionism; the Great Recession may end up eviscerating it.

categories of public employees collective-bargaining rights. Even if most government workers were stripped of collective-bargaining rights, they would retain more protections than private-sector workers, since most worker protections — such as merit-based hiring or the need for just cause to discipline or fire an employee – stem from civil-service laws passed well before collective-bargaining rights were put on the books. Government workers could still band together and exercise their rights as citizens by trying to elect politicians of their choice and by petitioning the government. Furthermore, much informal negotiation between the government and workers' representatives could still take place even if collective bargaining were not legally mandated. This in fact occurred in many states and cities prior to the adoption of collective-bargaining laws.

To weaken unions' political power in future negotiations, these reform-oriented governors have also sought to stop the government from collecting union dues. They aim to change the default option to one where workers wouldn't pay union dues unless they voluntarily decided to become a union member, even if they are covered by a union contract. This arrangement is called an open shop and currently exists in nearly half the states. Wisconsin currently has a closed shop, in which dues are automatically deducted from paychecks and workers must voluntarily opt out. The likely effect of the new laws in Ohio and Wisconsin will be to vastly reduce the amount of revenue the unions take in. In the long run, they would reduce membership, undermine a huge source of funds for Democrats, and reduce taxpayer support for a lobby that promotes larger government and more taxation. The Buckeye and Badger states are trying to provide a model for reform that would put their states on a path toward the saner and more responsible way of conducting government affairs, which was endorsed long ago by Franklin D. Roosevelt and George Meany.

Short of such a direct "assault," in President Obama's words, on the public unions, other governors have sought to work within existing arrangements toward similar ends. They have called for "shared sacrifice" to get public employees to contribute more toward their pension and health care plans, as they believe current commitments are untenable. "[Pension reform] is not a Democrat or

Republican issue," says Los Angeles Mayor Antonio Villaraigosa. "The fact is our pensions aren't sustainable." Villaraigosa is a former teachers-union organizer and a Democrat. He supports lowering pension benefits for new police officers and firefighters and requiring other public employees to pay more of their retirement health benefits. Another common proposal in this area is to stop governments from offering defined benefit plans and switch to defined contribution pension plans. The idea is to pay newer employees slightly more in salary and less in deferred pension and health care compensation. Reducing deferred payments has the virtue of reducing the number of opportunities politicians have to keep liabilities off the balance sheet. In 2010, public-employee unions in Vermont, Iowa, Minnesota, and Wyoming conceded to modest reductions in pension benefits. But more will need to be done to bring the states' pension funds into balance.

The difficulty with this approach is that calling for such reforms without touching unions' financial and political power leaves the dysfunctional relationships between public-employee unions, politicians, and the government intact. The unions can be counted on to make strategic sacrifices in the here and now to ensure that they can claw back losses when more favorable economic conditions return in the future. Consequently, the trouble with government unions is likely to persist in America's biggest Democratic strongholds.

In sum, we are likely to see a patchwork of reforms across the nation. Some states like Indiana and Wisconsin (and probably Ohio as well) have enacted deep reforms that weaken the political power of government unions in their states. Other states, like California, Pennsylvania, and New York, are likely to follow Chris Christie's model in New Jersey, demanding concessions from public-employee unions but leaving prevailing arrangements in place. The viability of either reform strategy will depend on the particular fiscal and political conditions in the states and cities.

The attack on reformers by the unions and

their defenders is designed to make any of the changes to current practice seem excessive. But by defending the status quo, when it means undermining the fiscal health and thereby the global power of the United States, the unions risk appearing irresponsible and selfish. The American people are now learning the dangers of handing over so much governing authority to unelected union officials whose interests are not synonymous with theirs. They must take the next step and pressure their elected representatives to take it back.

First American edition published in 2011 by Encounter Books,
an activity of Encounter for Culture and Education, Inc.,
a nonprofit, tax exempt corporation.
Encounter Books website address: www.encounterbooks.com

Manufactured in the United States and printed on
acid-free paper. The paper used in this publication meets
the minimum requirements of ANSI/NISO Z39.48–1992
(R 1997) (*Permanence of Paper*).

FIRST AMERICAN EDITION

LIBRARY OF CONGRESS CATALOGING-IN-PUBLICATION DATA

DiSalvo, Daniel.
Government unions and the bankrupting of America /
Daniel DiSalvo.
p. cm. — (Encounter broadsides)
ISBN-13: 978-1-59403-590-6 (pbk. : alk. paper)
ISBN-10: 1-59403-590-3 (pbk. : alk. paper)
1. Government employee unions—United States. 2. Collective
bargaining—Government employees—United States. I. Title.
HD8005.2.U5D58 2011
331.88 1135173—dc22
2011010704

10 9 8 7 6 5 4 3 2 1